A Life

Not Asked For

Kim Harris

HATCHBACK Publishing
Genesee Michigan

A Life Not Asked For
©2016 by Kim Harris

Published by HATCHBACK Publishing
Genesee, Michigan 48437
Since 2005

ISBN 978-1535371728

I have tried to recreate events, locales and conversations from my memories of them. In order to maintain their anonymity in some instances I have changed the names of individuals and places, I may have changed some identifying characteristics and details such as physical properties, occupations and places of residence. Details have been changed to protect the privacy of individuals.

Printed in the United States
10 9 8 7 6 5 4 3 2 1

For Worldwide Distribution

Dedication

I dedicate this book to all the children who feel they have no voice and to all those who are struggling with their past.

Acknowledgements

I would like to thank the members of the National Chapter of Aspiring Writers Association of America (AWAOA), who listened to my stories and never judged me but encouraged me. And last but not least I thank my husband for staying by my side and encouraging me to tell my story.

Content

Introduction

Every child depends on the love of family and children are supposed to be able to trust their love ones. I'm not really sure how old I was when my trust and love was betrayed by family. There are so many memories but the one that stays with me is being molested. As a child I spent a lot of time outside of this body that was given me. It became a ritual to disappear and stare into space, tuning out what was happening to me. After a while it all seemed normal, like a part of life. It's hard to distinguish right from wrong when you're being sexually molested by several men in one way or another, all of whom are your family or close to it. So many times I have tried to block the memories out of my head but there's no escaping what I have endured. My only options are to either let it consume me and lose or cope with it and survive.

So this is me. It is where I came from and what I've been through. It's my life as a child, a mother, a wife, and a Christian. This book is me, fighting to stay saved. As you read I pray you look at my life and although you may feel sorrow, or you may even feel my pain, that you get understanding most of all. Understand like I have come to understand that God doesn't put more on you than you can handle. Understand everything happens for a reason and though what we are going through is important, maybe even life changing, it is how we respond that makes the difference. Our response determines whether we win or lose. Understand that God gives us free will and though I have endured, I have chosen to fight. I pray that you choose to fight.

ONE

Lost Trust

Pulling my legs closely to my chest, hugging them tight, I rested my head on my knees as the water filled the tub. My mind is spinning out of control. Mr. Ware, Terry, Dan, I feel like that little girl that couldn't say no all those many years ago.

****

I live at 333 Park Street. I'm the fourth child of ten children, my name is Kim. There's my oldest sister and brothers Kesha, Derrick, Tony, then me. Then there's my younger siblings, Regina and Carl. Robert, Mary, John, and Chrissy are my father's children. They come over only on weekends, holidays, and whenever school is out, because they live with their mothers. We're all about two years apart in age except my baby sisters Mary and Regina, they are three months apart and Chrissy is the baby, she was born eleven years after Carl. Sometimes people think Regina and Mary are twins because they are the same age and are always dressed alike. Our house is big and we're the only ones on our street with a swimming pool in the back yard but we only have three bedrooms. My parents have their bedroom and Kesha has her own room too. She's lucky. I'm not sure who the last room belongs to but Derrick always gets the bed. Being one of the oldest has its perks I guess. The rest of us just end up wherever we fall asleep, which is usually in the living room on the couch or the floor. Mama works for General Motors, people call it GM. She works all the time, Monday through Friday and sometimes Saturdays too. Right now she's working second shift so she's gone from two o'clock in the afternoon until after twelve midnight, while dad spends all of his time at Arlene's bar. We call the bar his second home because that's where we usually find him when we need him. We have lots of fun, especially when Mom and Dad are gone. We play games like Monopoly and Tunk but Tony always wins. I think he cheats. Sometimes we end up fighting too, me and Tony mostly. From the outside looking in we probably look like a big family with lots of love but looks can be deceiving.

It's hot outside. Mom's not home and everyone else is playing up and down the street with their friends. Regina, Mary, and I are playing in the sandbox, well it's really a pile of dirt that sits outside in our yard. Daddy just pulled up and went into the house. When I went in to get some Kool-Aid, I went downstairs to the basement to see him. The room was dark and the only light is the daylight coming in through the windows. It smelled a little musty. Daddy was sitting on the bed, he said "Hey baby girl," and pulled me up on his lap. "You know Daddy loves you," he said and I nodded yes. He has his hand on my knee rubbing up and down my leg. I felt my panties being pulled to the side but I'm trying to concentrate on the light coming through the window and the laughter I hear outside. My sisters and brothers must be having fun. "If you tell anybody about this your Mother will get in trouble," he said as he lifted me off his lap and pulled a dollar out of his pocket. "Did you hear me?" I nodded yes again. He gave me a dollar and told me to go play.

I ran up the stairs going through the house so fast but when I got out the door Kesha stopped me on the porch. She said "What were you doing in the basement with Daddy?"

I hear her but all I'm thinking is I don't want Mama getting in trouble so I said, "Nothing. Daddy gave me a dollar," and I ran off the porch. This was the first time my trust was betrayed.

I love my sisters and brothers. It's so many of us we create our own fun most of the time. I'm not sure who started the water fight but I'm willing to bet it was Tony because he's always doing something. All I know is we're running around the house chasing each other with buckets of water. I'm all out so I got to get to the water hose and fill up but just as I got to the side of the house by the back door I got drenched with water. I didn't know how or who did it until I looked up and saw Tony and Robert hanging out the upstairs window yelling, "Gotcha'!" We have made such a mess. Water is everywhere, in and out of the house. We're always doing this but I wouldn't change having this kind of fun with them for anything.

Our block is full of families. The elderly couple, Mama Livey and Papa Jay live across the street and Derrick's friend, David, lives next door. Most of our neighbors think we're bad kids because there's always something going on at our house. If we're not playing with their children or ourselves, then we're fighting their children, or each other. Yesterday Tony and I were arguing and he chased me across the street to Mama Livey's house. I ran in and locked the door. She saw me coming because her and Papa Jay are always sitting in their recliners in the window watching everything that goes on. She yelled out the door and told Tony to leave me alone and go home. She gave me some Lemonheads and I sat over there until Kesha or Derrick got home. Kesha and Derrick helps her and Papa Jay with their daily living like house cleaning and yard work. They give them money for helping out. Sometimes she will have me do little things around the house when I'm over there like find a gown for her or put her food in the ice box and she will give me fifty cents for doing it.

Tony and I are always feuding. Maybe it's because we're so close in age. I'm not sure but he play's too much and is always messing with me. One thing I will say about my siblings, we are always there for each other, especially when it comes to one of us getting into a fight with someone else, which happens more than usual around here. Tony just got chased home after school by a group of kids and usually Derrick is home to run them away but this time our dog Alfie was in the yard tied to the tree. Alfie is an Afghan and he stands as tall as a horse. Tony made it home and yelled out to Alfie, he stood up and Tony untied him from the tree. Everyone who chased Tony home turned around and ran back up the street. Tony is always aggravating somebody so it wasn't unusual for him to get chased home. We call him a nerd because he's very smart and I think he likes showing off. He really gets on my nerves.

****

It's late and I'm the only person woke. Mama always brings home pop bottles and whoever is still up when she gets there, gets to have them. I always try to stay woke so I can get them and cash them in at the store for money. Tonight Daddy was home in his room and I was in the living room waiting for Mama to call. Right at two o'clock in the morning the phone rang and I answered it. Knowing it was Mama I said, "Hi Mama." She asked was Daddy home, I said yes and took him the phone. When he hung up he told me to get my shoes on I was going with him to pick Mama up. I was happy because I finally get to see where Mama worked. It's dark and quiet in the car and barely any other cars on the road. Daddy turned on this street that looks even darker than the main streets. He pulled into a church parking lot. I'm not sure why because Mama works in a shop, not a church. He unzipped his pants, put his hand on my head and pulled me down, and told me to put it in my mouth. When he let me go he reached into the glove compartment, gave me some Listerine, told me to gargle with it, and spit it out. Then he pulled down the street and picked Mama up. Many nights after that whenever he was home, I would fake like I'm sleep in the room with my brothers.

Aside from tuning out what was happening to me, I try to escape by spending as much time as I can over a friend's house. It's a whole other world for me around the corner over her house. What's really cool is we share the same name and our numerical addresses are the same too, just different streets. When I go over her house I can't help but wish I could stay. She and her sister have so many toys. At dinner time they go sit at the table and eat. It is so different from what goes on at my house. My Mama cooks the dinner before she leaves for work and throughout the day everybody eats whenever they want. Sometimes if we want something different, like fries, we cook it ourselves. I accidently set the kitchen on fire once because I forgot the grease was getting hot so I could cook some fries. Maybe my friend and her family are able to do things differently than us because it's only two of them and ten of us. Whatever the reason, I want to be part of it.

Mama is gone to the store with my Auntie and Daddy didn't come home last night. Mary and Robert's brother, Joe, is over our house. He's around the same age as one of my older brothers. We call him our brother too since we share the same siblings. It's early in the afternoon and as I was coming downstairs from my sister's room where I wasn't supposed to be because she told me to stay out. Joe was sitting in the living room watching television and he stopped me as I was heading out the door telling me to come here.

"Where are you going," he said.

"I'm going outside to find Mary and Regina," I

responded.

"I know what your dad be doing to you," he said.

I'm afraid to speak. *God I wish I would have went outside when everybody else did but no I had to go in Kesha's room being nosey.* Tuning him out, I ran out the door.

TWO

No Voice

You would think that I liked watching cartoons because that's what children do. Not me. I'm more drawn to movies about molestation or rape. To this day I still desire these types of movies. Don't get me wrong, as a child I did play a lot but my interest when it came to television was different. A friend of mine once said all I was doing was reliving the hurt over and over again every time I watch these movies. Maybe she's right but I also believe it's because I can relate to the victims. They are me and I am them.

It's late in the evening and Mama is sleep on her bed. She always falls asleep fully dressed watching TV with no cover. It seems like her bed is always covered with clothes. My little sisters are sleep on Mama's bedroom floor. Not sure who else besides Tony is woke but since he's already watching the TV in the living room, I'm just going to lay down on the floor next to Mary and Regina and watch a good movie until I fall asleep. The light is off and I must be more tired than I thought because I kept nodding in and out on this movie. I could still smell the aroma of the tacos Mama cooked earlier. Her tacos be so good. I must have really dosed off because now it's the end of the movie and I'm laying here staring at the blue carpet wishing I stayed woke. Then I heard a woman's voice on the television saying, "If you or anyone you know is a victim of child molestation please call." I looked up and a hotline number appeared across the TV screen. I checked on Mama. She was still sleeping and my sisters were too. I stared at that number, memorizing it and wanting badly to call it. I got up and left Mama's room repeating the number under my breath. When I got to the phone, I dialed the numbers as I repeated them in my head. I stopped and hung the phone up. I couldn't do it. I just balled up on the corner of the couch and fell asleep.

I found myself always thinking of ways to tell someone what was happening to me and then chickening out. I just wanted somebody to know but I didn't want to be the one to tell. I would find myself imagining while looking at magazines, cutting out letters from different words to form the words I wanted to say but I could never bring myself to do it. I don't know how to bring myself to say the words, "I'm being molested by my father." *What would people think about me? Will they be mad at me? And what about my mother, is she going to get in trouble?* I was scared and confused.

The next day before Dad took Mama to work I asked her if I could spend the night over my friend

Kelly's house and she agreed. I'm not sure where everyone else was but I was getting ready to leave when David from next door came over asking for Derrick. I told him I don't know then I went to see if he was in the bedroom. Coming back into the living room I told David he wasn't home and when I sat on the couch to call Kelly, he sat down next to me. Trying to ignore him because this seemed all too familiar, when Kelly answered I asked her to meet me half way because she lived three blocks away. She agreed and I hung up the phone. Still sitting next to me, David grabbed my hand when I went to get up and said "You are so pretty." I sat there saying nothing. *Here we go again.* I felt his hand go under my shorts and he put his finger in my private part. *Where is everybody? As many people that live in this house and come and go, how does this keep happening to me?* He finally stopped. It seemed like forever but it couldn't have been because Kelly only lives about ten minutes away and when I heard the doorbell ring I knew it was her. He didn't say anything. He just got up and left out the door. I grabbed my bag, left with Kelly and walked back to her house. I must have a sign on my back that reads: *Here I am. Come molest me.*

****

It's the summer before I start middle school and Kesha is moving out of town to live with my grandmother but I don't want her to go. I never told her what was happening to me but I still felt like her leaving left me all alone. I looked up to her. She's so pretty and cool but now she's gone and I am so mad at her for leaving me here. Over the next few years my father continued to molest me. Many nights I was awakened out of my fake sleep and had to perform oral sex on him. He would say, "When you are old enough we will go all the way." My desire to tell someone just disappeared and this is what life was to me.

Dad's friend Sherry and her little girl moved in and they slept in the basement. Sherry was really cool. I got to go with her to the store and other places. I spent a lot of time in the basement hanging with her and her daughter. She was like another big sister until I found out why she was really there. It was late and I was in the bedroom with my brothers. They were sleep and I was waiting up as usual for Mama to come home with the bottles. Dad was home which is why I went to the bedroom with my brothers and when I heard someone in the hallway I pretended to be sleep on the floor. With my head turned away from the door and my eyes closed, I just listened. The bedroom door opened and then closed. I just laid there for a few minutes with eyes still closed and my head pressed against the orange carpet, listening to the TV. When I finally opened my eyes, I turned around to finish watching TV in the dark. I was careful to keep quiet, ready to close my eyes quickly if Dad came back. While laying there waiting for Mama to call, I kept hearing something but couldn't make out what it was so I reached up and turned the television down and listened for the sound again. I got up and opened the door really slow peeping into the hallway. From there I could hear the sound more clearly. The hallway is very small, like a little circle. From it you can see my parent's room, the bedroom I'm in, the bathroom, and the living room. The sound was coming from the living room. The voice was very low. It was Sherry and my daddy. They are on the couch and she keeps saying "Yes." Daddy and Sherry was having sex. I stepped back into the bedroom and pulled the door to but I didn't close it. I laid back down but I started crying very quietly. I wanted them to stop and when they heard me they did. I saw Sherry coming to the room. I closed my eyes but she noticed I was faking and pulled the door back. When the phone rang I knew it was Mama. Sherry came to the room and asked me if I wanted to go with her to pick my Mama up from work. I was still dressed so I just put on my shoes and we left.

The car ride was quiet but not for long. "Did you hear me and your daddy?" Sherry asked.

"Yes," I answered.

"Why were you crying?" she asked. I didn't answer her. After a few more minutes of silence she then asked, "Are you jealous? Do you want your daddy to do that to you?"

Is that what I wanted? I saw them having sex. Why is he doing this to Mama? If he has women then why is he messing with me? Now I'm having feelings of jealousy toward Sherry. I started crying. I'm so confused.

****

One day my siblings and I were all in the house playing and the new neighbors who moved in next door after David and his family moved, came over. When we answered the door, the man asked had we seen his son and we said no. His son was around five years old and we never knew him to leave the yard. He started walking down the street looking for his son so we decided to help. We looked up and down the block calling his name. Daddy pulled up and asked us what we were doing. We told him the neighbor's son was lost and we were helping him look for him. Daddy started helping us look for the little boy. He walked toward the back of our house to see if the little boy had gotten in our backyard. The fence was opened. This time of year it was cold enough for ice to form over the top of the water in our pool. He entered the pool area and there was a crack in the ice. My dad could see the floating body of the little boy. Our neighbor's son drowned in our pool that day. Shortly after that my parents decided to move. We left Park Street and Sherry did not come with us.

****

I'm turning fifteen years old and having a birthday party at our new house. It is going to be in the basement. When we left our old neighborhood, my friendship with Kim and Kelly became distant. I haven't made friends with new people in this neighborhood yet so my party only consisted of family members, my siblings and cousins. I'm having so much fun dancing although I can't dance a lick. I'm just happy they are here to celebrate with me. I can't remember ever having a birthday party. Mom's home and Dad's not. Everything is perfect.

Our new house seems bigger than our last house. We still only have three bedrooms. This time the boys share a room and me and my younger sisters share a room. It's only a one story house but the basement is finished and it has a bar. Dad has al-

already thrown a few parties down there and tonight he's giving another one. People are coming and going while I'm trying to watch TV in the living room. My sisters are in our room playing and my brothers are in their room watching television too. Some man I didn't know came upstairs. I thought he was going out the door but he came over and sat on the couch across from me. I went to get up to leave but he jumped up in front of me and just stood there. I froze for a second and he sat back down right next to me. The door to our basement slides back and forth to open and close so when I heard it open from the kitchen, I knew someone was coming. He got up at the sound and left out the front door. My heart was beating fast as I ran down our long hallway. My room was the first one on the left, then there were two linen closets. Across from each closet was my parents' room on the left and my brothers' room on the right. The bathroom was at the very end of the hall. I ran in and closed the door. Sitting on the floor up against the door crying, my heart was still pounding. I stayed there until someone knocked on the door to use the bathroom.

****

A few days later the weather was nice. I was getting ready to go down the street to one of my new friend's house. Dad was outside sitting in the yard playing chess with one of his friends.

I was just walking out the door when Uncle Ralph pulled up in his new Cadillac. He's Dad's favorite uncle. He drops everything when Uncle Ralph calls him. He was getting out the car when I was walking off the porch.

"Hi Uncle Ralph," I said. I went to give him a hug and a kiss on the cheek like I always have since I was little but this time he turned his head and kissed me on the lips. I felt his tongue touch my lips. Instantly feeling guilty, I just walked off and from that day forward I decided to steer clear of him. I was living in a new house, I was in a different neighborhood but I found my environment hadn't changed.

THREE

Strength Unknown

It's my last year of high school, Kesha moved back home over a year ago. Derrick moved out before we even moved from Park Street because of the incident between him and Daddy. One night around ten o'clock Daddy came home after being gone all day. He hadn't even called to see if Mama needed to go anywhere or needed anything. He pulled up and left his girlfriend Jade in the car. When Dad came in the house, drunk as usual, Mama was mad at him. She started arguing with him and they went back and forth until Mama said, "I'm tired of this shit."

Dad must of did something to make Derrick think he was about to hit Mama because Derrick stood up and jumped in between them. Daddy backed down and left that night. I was told the next night while Derrick and his girlfriend were sitting in his car in the driveway, Daddy knocked on the window and asked him to step out the car for a minute. When Derrick got out the car Daddy pulled a knife on him and told him if he ever jumped in him and Mama's business again he would kill him. Derrick told Daddy that he was moving out because he better not ever see him hit Mama. So Derrick moved right down the street to our Auntie's house.

I didn't get to walk with the rest of my class because I had to do one more semester, so I wouldn't officially graduate until January. Despite all the years of betrayal from men, I really liked this boy name Geon. I met him the year before at a skating rink. When   I saw his picture, somehow I knew we were going to be friends. I just felt it. On his graduation night he could have been doing anything else but he came to see me. We shared our first kiss. After a year of talking on and off on the phone we finally made it official and he became my boyfriend.

I've never been in a real relationship. I have had one or two boyfriends before him but I kept them at bay. I would talk on the phone with them and might even go visit them but in my mind boys were cheaters and they just wanted one thing from girls. Watching my Dad cheat on my mother for so many years gave me that impression. Geon broke through the barrier I built around me without even knowing there was one to break through. For some reason he seemed different. He made me laugh.

The summer was going by fast. My last semester of school was approaching quickly. Having Geon as my boyfriend was like another life than what I was used to. One day I walked over to his cousin's house to see him and they asked me to cook some chicken. I didn't know the first thing about cooking chicken but I didn't tell them that. I just put some cooking grease in a pot, took the chicken wings out of the ice box and when the grease got hot, I dropped the chicken in the pot. When they browned I took them out because they looked done. He had his mouth all ready but when he bit into the chicken, it was still bleeding. It was funny.

Late that night I got off the phone with Geon. Everyone's sleep but me and I'm hungry. Fries are one thing I knew how to cook because we cooked them all the time. I decided to make me some. I heard the door open and could hear Daddy coming in the house. He went to his room and when I finished cooking my fries, I hoped he had fell asleep but he didn't. I took my food to my room and closed the door but he came in looking for me.

"It's time. You're old enough for us to go all the way," he said.

I froze for what felt like a long time. While looking away, staring at the floor covered with clothes and toys, I managed to zero in on the green carpet and said "No!" Afraid of what was coming next, I sat there holding my plate of fries. He left my room and never touched me again.

I turned eighteen year old a few months later in

November. Geon and I had gotten closer, so close in fact I found out I was pregnant. I was only about one month. When I told my mother and she told everybody else. She thought I got pregnant losing my virginity on my eighteen birthday. I decided to let her continue believing that. Truth is, aside from my innocence being taken, not by actual intercourse, I lost my virginity last year while trying to impress a boy by drinking with him. I got so drunk I couldn't even remember having sex. I also lost my rings I had bought for myself that night. I didn't really care what anybody said. I thought of Geon as my first because with him is where I felt something for the first time. He didn't make me feel dirty, guilty, or scared.

One morning I woke up feeling pains in my stomach. I was nervous because I was only a little over a month pregnant. Geon took me to the hospital. We were waiting for the doctor to come in and examine me. When she came in, she explained to us she was going to listen for the baby's heartbeat. She lifted my shirt and squirted some type of jelly substance on my belly. She used some object to listen to the baby only there was no sound. The doctor turns off the machine and tells us she believes the baby is dead in my womb and she will need to perform a D&C on me. Just like that our baby was gone. I wasn't really sure how to feel.

All I knew, one minute there was a life growing inside of me and the next it wasn't. The car ride home was quiet when Geon dropped me off at home. Once everyone left me alone I laid on the couch and cried until I fell asleep.

Two weeks had passed since my miscarriage. School had resumed from the Christmas break. My last semester of high school was coming to an end and all I had left to do was take my finals which started the next day. Then I would be done. I usually stayed up late but I decided to try and go to sleep early because I had finals in the morning. Daddy walked in and Sherry was with him. He started fussing about the house not being clean so Regina and I started cleaning up.

He was drunk. He came in the kitchen where I was and said, "Go help with the living room."

"I'm washing the dishes," I answered.

He slapped me and said, "This is my house and as long as you live here, you will do what I say!"

Looking him in his face I said, "You just gave me a reason to move out of your house!" I walked off heading to my room.

He was walking behind me, pushing me down the hall yelling, "Who do you think you are?"

Once we got to my room, which was at the end of the hall now because my big brothers were gone, he pushed me in the room. He came in, closed and locked the door so no one could get in.

"You think you cute!" He hit me again.

I reached on the dresser, grabbed the iron and swung it at him. It startled him when I hit him back. Throwing me down on the bed, he got on top of me, pinning my arms down with his knees so I couldn't hit him again. Yelling he said, "You think you cute getting pregnant!" He kept hitting me in my face. Suddenly he stopped and got up off me. While walking out of my room he said, "Clean your face up!"

When I came out of my room he was in his room and Sherry was gone. Regina must have been in her room with Carl because I didn't see her. I grabbed the phone and went down to the basement. I called the police and told them I was just beaten and gave them our address. I hung up the phone and went back upstairs to finish washing the dishes. When someone knocked on the door, I heard Dad answer it.

"Sir we got a call about somebody being beaten," the police said.

"Nothing's going on here," I heard him say.

I knew they were getting ready to leave so I stepped out from the kitchen so the police could see me. Looking at my face they said "Are you the person who called us?"

"Yes," I answered.

"Do you want to tell us what happened?"

Daddy was staring at me. I asked if they would take me over my sister's house and they said yes. The police dropped me off over to my step-siblings' house.

When Kesha came home I got dropped back off. By the time I got there, the police had been called back and they ended up arresting Daddy on a gun possession charge. Mama happened to be working a longer shift and didn't get off work until five o'clock in the morning. When she walked in the house she came back to my room where my Auntie, my sisters, and I were talking. She knew Dad was in jail and when she walked in, my Auntie started telling her about what he did to me. Mama was sitting there just taking everything in and not saying anything.

Out of nowhere I said, "Daddy has been making me do things to him."

The tension in the room was obvious. My Auntie

broke the silence. "What was he making you do?"

Staring at the orange carpet I said, "He puts his thing in my mouth."

"Oh no!" my Auntie said.

Staring at the wall I continued, "And he's been doing this to me since I was little."

"Why didn't you tell somebody?" my Auntie said.

"I couldn't. He said Mama would get in trouble if I told anybody." The sun was coming up and shining between the orange and brown curtains on my window. I was tired and went to lay back on my bed.

"You get some sleep while me and your Mama go talk," my Auntie said.

Everybody left my room and I was alone. Staring out into the room, not looking at anything in particular, I finally fell asleep.

The phone ringing woke me up. Realizing I missed my final exams, I jumped up and called Geon to come and get me. I hadn't talked to him so he didn't know my Daddy jumped on me during the night. When he saw my face he was instantly upset asking me what happened. I told him what my Dad did to me and everything he said.

Geon said, "So he jumped on you because you got pregnant?"

I needed to get to the school before it closed because it was a half day due to finals and I wanted to let them know why I wasn't able to take my finals.

"Will you please take me to school and I will tell you everything on the way," I said.

When we got in the car I told him what my dad had been doing to me all these years. I wasn't sure how he was going to react but I was tired of this secret. I didn't think I had anymore tears. To my surprise he hugged me and I started crying because I thought once I told him he would leave and run as far away from me as possible, but he didn't.

He grabbed me, held me close and said, "It's going to be okay."

FOUR

Finding My Own Way

I decided to press charges against Dad for jumping on me. The judge ordered a restraining order that stated he had to stay one hundred yards away from me. He moved in with his mother in her apartment. When he was asked how he survived financially, he stated his wife worked. The judge told him to get a job and he did. I think he started washing dishes at a local restaurant. Mama walks down to the corner from our house to meet him because of the restraining order. I didn't really know how to feel about that and I couldn't dwell on it because I had to prepare for finals. After explaining to the school why I didn't make it to take the finals, they agreed to let me take them on another day.

I graduated high school and got my first job as an adult, working in a Direct Care home. I also found out I was pregnant. I was so excited. I was still living at home with Mama but I spent most of my time over Geon's grandmother's house with him. Mom's shift at GM goes until five thirty in the morning now and I started picking her up since Dad was still living with Grandma. I thought it best especially since I was pregnant again and he wouldn't have to come to the house.

The months came and went fast. I was big as a house but I loved feeling this little one inside of me and watching my stomach as the baby moved around. We had a month to go before our baby was born and I had to find a house for us. I wasn't planning on moving until Dad convinced Mama to ask me to go to the court and speak on his behalf. Apparently his probation officer or somebody told him if his victim was okay with it, he could get the restraining order removed. He wanted me to tell them that I had no problem with him coming back home. The only problem with that was I did. Not having him around had been different in a good way. Going through the day without having to see him bringing women back to the house cheating on Mama, in our faces, and not caring how we felt, I thought she'd be relieved not to have to deal with his mess. I told her I would do it but I decided to move so I wouldn't be the reason they were not together.

A few weeks had gone by since Mama asked me to speak on Dad's behalf so he could come back home. I had been looking for a house so I could move and had finally found one. It was small, only a two bedroom. We could literally see the back door from the front door and all the other rooms. Everything was just a step away. The beds are the only thing that fit in the bedrooms. This was my first house and the only thing we could afford. Geon and I moved together. I was excited and scared at the same time. I didn't know what kind of mother I would be.

All I knew was what I had been through and I didn't want to bring a baby into a world like that. I wasn't sure who I was or what I was capable of. I couldn't protect myself from it so I didn't know how I was going to protect someone else. I didn't know what I was doing and the more I thought about it, I didn't want to go through with it, but it was too late. My due date was close.

FIVE

I Let Go of My Security Blanket

I am so tired of everybody putting me in this box expecting me to always do things the right way. Everyone thinks they know me and if I so much as step one foot outside the box they have me in, they act like I broke the law or something. They all expect me to be nice, sweet Kim, the one who's always there for them. The one who never says no when they need something. If you need a babysitter call Kim. If you need a ride call Kim. Kim is a sweetheart. She doesn't go out, she doesn't drink, she's faithful, and a good person. Why can't I for once go out and have fun and not care? Why can't I be the unpredictable one for a change? If I turn my phone off I get messages like: *Where are you? This is not like you. Why aren't you answering your phone?* Out of my four sisters, I am the married one so they don't spend as much time with me as they do with each other. They hang out together all the time at clubs or at each other's houses. *God I'm tired of caring. Everyone else is doing what they want without a care in the world so why can't I?*

Geon and I have been married eight years now and have three children. We have had our share of arguments over the years but lately it has been the worst of the worst. We go to sleep and wake up angry at each other. Recently he threw my ring across the street and a day later I found my wedding dress hanging in the closet ruined, cut down the middle. I sat up late one night watching television in the living room with the lights off. I began to dwell on how we got here. I know it's not that we fell out of love. I still love him and I know he loves me but we both have our defenses up and we're hurting one another because of it. I look at how he keeps hiring different women to work in his office without even consulting me and I feel disrespected and when I express it, he gets defensive. And then there's this club promotion stuff he's doing with his friends that keeps him out at night. I know all too well what that life leads to and it's not where I want to be. I watched my Dad cheat on my mother hanging out at the club every night, bringing women to our home calling them friends, kissing them in front of us, and not caring at all that we saw it. I can't and won't go through that. The club is where it starts and he's not taking my feelings into consideration. All he keeps saying is, "I'm not your dad." It's gotten so I don't even want to talk to him.

Staring at the beautiful hardwood floor and looking around at everything we've accomplished, I am determined to move our children out of the environment we were brought up in. We bought our first home in a beautiful neighborhood across town. God knows I don't want to leave but after last night I have to go before something bad happens.

I'm overwhelmed with the thoughts of living without him. Even though it was dark, I could see myself cutting my wrist as if I had a razor in my hand deciding which way I should go, up and down or across. I didn't think giving my life to Christ would be this way. The day I got saved I thought all my troubles would go away but it's been just the opposite. It felt like I was always fighting something but it is my walk in this journey that gave me the strength to rebuke the thoughts of killing myself. The only way I knew how to survive was to remove myself from the situation. I needed to leave but I was not walking away. I understood leaving will either bring us back together or break us a part for good. I was willing to take that chance, hoping that he sees what's more important and we find the love we had for one another.

I was able to move out. I sold my first house as a Realtor and got a really good commission. In the beginning when I moved, I felt what seemed like a tremendous amount of stress released. It was like I could breathe again and not have to deal with constantly arguing with Geon. He and I decided to have the kids stay with each of us every other week. Everything was going fine. Geon and I were getting along. He would spend the night from time to time. So much for being separated. It didn't last long. This was my first year as a Realtor and I hadn't sold anything since the big sale that made it possible for me to move, and that was over a month ago.

I told Geon I needed help paying bills but he said he needed to pay his own bills. He saw me struggling yet he came over, spent nights with me having sex, and eating as if we were a family. He was paying bills at his house and not even trying to help me. I think he's purposely not helping me financially in hopes that I would give up and go back home. This made me so angry. Instead of giving up, I became more determined to prove him wrong. So aside from my career as a Realtor, I started working first shift for a theater producer as an assistant.

Working for the producer was cool at first but I was still barely making ends meet and it was Christmas time. After paying my rent, I was completely broke and I couldn't buy my children anything for Christmas. I wasn't asking Geon for anything. When I made it to the theater my boss, Mr. Ware, wasn't in yet so I got busy creating a mailing list for play announcements. No one else worked there and I was all alone. All I kept thinking about was being able to give my babies a Christmas.

Mr. Ware arrived and I continued to work across from him in this tiny room he called an office that sat in the basement of a church. It was only big enough for two desks. Aside from a few phone calls he made, it was so quiet you can hear a pin drop. The day finally came to an end and it was almost time for me to go. I had to catch the bus home so I started to wrap things up and seal my last few envelopes.

"You look like something's wrong," Mr. Ware said. I just slowly nodded my head as if to say nothing's wrong.

Then he said, "You look like somethings on your mind."

I told him I was stressing about not being able to afford to buy my kids anything for Christmas. Just as I was getting up from my desk, he got up, came over and stood in front of me. He put his hands around me hugging me. I just stood there silently while he said, "You are so pretty."

The silence seemed like it went on forever but it didn't. He quickly followed up with, "I can give you an advance so you can give your children a Christmas."

I was kind of surprised yet waiting for the other catch and then he said it.

"You have to do something for me."

The silence filled the room as he continued to stand there with his arm around me. Then he let me go and asked did I want the advancement and I said yes. Noticing that I missed the bus he said he would take me home so he wrote me a check for the advancement and left. Instead of taking me home, he rode far out on Port Highway and pulled into this motel. He left me in the car for a second and sitting there I was dazed. *This isn't happening. What am I doing?* He got back in the car and drove just around the back to one of the rooms and we got out of the car and went in.

I just sold myself for one hundred and fifty dollars. How did I get here?

He took me home and I never returned to work after that day.

Christmas Eve came and my children was over Geon's house. He's going to drop them off later so that gave me enough time to go Christmas shopping. I managed to make that one hundred fifty dollars go a long way. With the boys being older, they didn't want a lot of toys so I got both of them cell phones and they were content. I spent the rest of the money buying toys for my daughter. Even though the most of the gifts were for her, they all were excited just to see gifts under the tree. I was so happy to see them smiling considering all they had been through watching their father and I separate and having to go back and forth living with us. Not to mention the stress they saw me going through trying to pay bills on my own.

Since I stopped working for the theater producer, I started the position of receptionist that was being offered at the real estate firm I was licensed through. That was still not enough to survive, so I applied for a job at Meijer's and also at a Direct Care home. I got hired at both. I started working a first, second, and third shift job. I am determined to show Geon that I can do this without his help. If working three jobs was what it took then I had to do what I had to do. I refused to ever resort to doing what I did to give my children a Christmas. Every time I thought about what I did, I felt anger in my heart, not for me but for Geon. Every time he came over, I felt hatred building up so much I started hanging out in clubs with my sisters. I had to get my mind off of everything. I just grew more angry every time I saw him.

This is about the second time I had been out with my sisters and though they still had me in this little box, it's okay. I was just enjoying spending time with them. Some guy once tried to buy me a drink and my sister told him I didn't drink. He looked at me crazy. I just smiled and waited for my chance to play pool. My sisters introduced to me this guy named Terry. Apparently he wanted to meet me. They said he's a good guy and he did appear to be a standup guy, tall dark skin, clean cut. Standing there in his black slacks and button up shirt, he says, "I didn't know they had another sister, where have you been hiding?" I told him I was married but separated. He seemed a little concerned yet still interested enough to keep talking to me. Being frustrated with my husband, I decided to try and push Geon away and figured this would be the best way to get over him. Even though I was angry with him I still loved him. I just needed to do something that would help me forget about him. I was tired of thinking about it. I'd been going out with my sisters and I really hadn't been having fun. I was sitting there watching their purses and their drinks, and watching them have fun. So I ordered a drink, nothing too strong, just a cooler, and I did it. I gave Terry my phone number and to my surprise he called me.

After talking to him for a little over a month, it seemed all he wanted was sex. We only saw each other when we were both out at the same time and then he wanted me to go back to his house. When I asked about us doing anything else like going out to eat or movies, he said he didn't want to because I was married. Changing the conversation, I asked him if I could borrow one hundred dollars because I needed to pay a bill and he said yes he would lend it to me. After that conversation I didn't hear from him for a week.

When my sisters and I went out another night and I didn't see him. I assumed he just wasn't coming. I decided to walk through the front of the club since it wasn't my turn to play pool and I looked over and there he was sitting with a woman at the front. He saw me coming through. Looking in his face as I'm walking, I maneuvered around people, and reached his table. I nodded and kept going. I stopped talking to him and shortly after my sister introduced me to another man. He lived out of town but visited here regularly. I'm not really sure why all these different men were interested in me but it was taking my mind off Geon. I thought that was what I needed. This guy was interesting. He said he was a bounty hunter. He's older, looks like he's in his fifties. His name was Dan. After going out to eat and to the clubs all week, he left town but asked me to visit him next month.

Now that he's gone I have been trying to avoid Geon all week but with Dan going back home and me not talking to Terry anymore, it's almost impossible. Geon found out about Dan because one of my relatives called him and told him. He questioned me about him. He had been coming around all week constantly trying to do something for me. I'm frustrated with him so tonight, after having a few drinks and seeing him out at the club, I came back to my house and just unloaded on him. I was crying and begging him to please leave me alone and he finally left.

I haven't seen or heard from Geon all week. I don't know why I'm worrying about what he's doing. I have been content with talking to Dan on the phone, since he lives out of town, and going out with my sisters having a drink and playing pool has been fun. Its three o'clock in the morning and my mind is still on what Geon is doing. I put my shoes on, got in my car and went over to his house. I knew the back door would be unlocked because the latch was broken. I went in and walked through the dark up to what used to be our bedroom. Anticipating seeing a girl in bed with him, I opened the door slowly and peeped in. He was sleep, alone. I quietly pulled his door back, left and went home.

I had been seeing Terry out but we hadn't spoken to each other and I was cool with that. Dan called me one night to tell me that he lived with a woman but they are no longer together. I asked him why he didn't tell me this in the beginning. *Because you wanted to use me just like every other man in my life and telling me would mess that up.* I hung up the phone. Shortly after hanging up with Dan my phone rang. It was Terry. I'm not really sure why he's calling me. I just saw him out at the club a couple of hours ago but we hadn't talked.

"Terry why are you calling me?"

"Who was that man you were with all last week?" he asked.

"Really? You called me at two o'clock in the morning because you want to know who I've been seeing! What do you really want Terry?"

"I want to see you," he said.

"You just saw me a couple of hours ago," I said.

"I want to see you now. Can I come pick you up?" he asked.

"Why Terry? You decided you didn't want to be with me back when I saw you with that girl."

"You're married."

"But we're separated and going through a divorce. I told you this," I said.

"Can I come pick you up? I want to see you."

Before I knew it I said yes. The car ride was quiet and as soon as we got to his house, it was routine as usual. He led me straight to his bedroom.

Why am I here? Why can't I say no? When it was over, I got up and went to the bathroom.

Pulling my legs closely to my chest, hugging them tight, I rested my head on my knees as the water filled the tub. My mind was spinning out of control. Mr. Ware, Terry, Dan, I felt like that little girl that couldn't say no all those many years ago. The tears wouldn't stop. I got dressed and asked him to take me home.

When I got in my apartment I went to my room and fell on my bed crying, "God this isn't me. This isn't my life. Help me God please. No matter how many jobs I get I can't make ends meet. My children were used to one way of life and I have exposed them to other lifestyles and behaviors. I can't take this anymore. I'm broken and lost God. I pushed my husband away by sleeping with these men and God I feel like he was my security blanket.

I can't do this anymore. Why is this happening to me?"

   As I laid there and began to fall asleep a voice came to me as if someone was in the room...*You asked for this.*

SIX

Skeletons

I laid there until the wee hours of the morning. It was still dark outside. I was thinking about what I had done over these last few months and then realized today was the last day of our reconciliation period to make our divorce final. I was tired of this merry go round. I mustard up the courage to call Geon. I knew he was sleep and wasn't sure if he would answer the phone because I hadn't talked to him in well over a week.

When he answered I quickly said, "Please come and get me."

The only questioned he asked was, "Where are you?"

When he got there, I locked the door on my way out and I never saw that apartment again. Geon held me in his arms until daylight came. When I woke up he was already gone to work so I just laid there taking in the fact I was back to a familiar place, our bedroom. I got up and walked through the house. I couldn't help but feel relieved. My children were sleeping in their bedrooms and it felt like I never left. I was home.

I'm so grateful God restored what I thought I destroyed. A day doesn't go by that I don't think about what I did. I committed adultery and I can't change that. I have asked for forgiveness but I can't help but wonder about how or when I will have to pay for what I've done. *Thou shalt not commit adultery* is the seventh commandment and it is written in the Bible that it is one of the sins which God dealt with harshly. I go to sleep and dream about Geon cheating on me constantly.

We renewed our vows and our bond seems closer than ever. We look at life differently now. He gave his life to Christ and I rededicated my life to Christ and together we have been doing this one day at a time.

****

Sometime later at one my doctor's appointments while waiting for my results from my annual physical, the doctor told me my white blood cells were slightly low and prescribed vitamins. He said he would recheck it on my next visit. I thought nothing of it. After some months I realized I missed my appointment so I rescheduled. That Sunday before I was due to go back to the doctor, I was sitting in church next to my mother and she had just finished her testimony.

"I'm cold," she said to me.

"It's not cold to me but let me check the other side of the room," I answered.

I got up, walked just about three steps across from where Mom was sitting. Testimony service was still going. I looked back at Mama and she was rubbing her arm up and down.

I walked over to her and said, "It's a little warmer on that side so let's move over there."

I reached to help her get her things and she said her arm felt funny. I instantly knew something was wrong so I shouted, "Someone call 911! I think Mama is having a stroke or a heart attack!"

Everyone stopped and my brother Derrick, who is our Pastor, rushed over to us. He grabbed Mama as she began to lean over on the pew.

"Derrick, I'm scared," Mama said.

"I got you Mama. I hear the ambulance pulling down the street," Derrick replied.

My husband directed them in while we all grabbed our things. I got in the ambulance with Mama and everybody else followed to the hospital. We waited for hours, all of us, my siblings, my father, my aunties and uncles, and cousins. In a private waiting room the doctor tells us she has suffered a stroke and she's in a coma.

My whole week turned into going back and forth to the hospital daily. I forgot again about my appointment. With all this going on I just didn't reschedule.

It's been seven months and Mom hasn't woke up. They have moved her from one hospital to another and now she's in a nursing home. We were taking turns sitting with her every day until we got a call from the nursing home that she stopped breathing, CPR was started but she was down for a long time. They rushed her to the hospital and wanted to meet with the family. When we got to the hospital the doctor told us she was down for some time before they brought her back and the machines are doing all the work. Also, she's not initiating anything and we needed to make a decision to keep her on the machines or turn them off and let her rest in peace.

We decided to turn the machines off at two o'clock in the afternoon. It would give everybody enough time to go and get their children out of school so we all can be with her when they unplugged her. We were all standing around her bed. My Grandmother led a gospel hymn and as we were singing, the doctor unplugged the machine. She told us she would stop breathing within a few minutes. We're singing during this transition but

Mama continued to breathe on her own. Thirty minutes passed and the doctor came in and we're still singing.

"I don't know what to say," the doctor replied. She left the room.

Late in the evening and some family members left but my aunties, Derrick, a few cousins, and myself stayed there over night with Mama. When morning came, she was still breathing. Hospice came in and asked if we wanted to take her home. I set it up for Mama to go home to my Grandmother's house. I didn't want her going back to her house. Dad was there. He may have thought we didn't know he and his last girlfriend were back to sleeping with each other while our mother was on her death bed but we knew. I didn't want my Mama around that environment. After all the equipment was set up at Grandma's house, I found a baby mattress in the basement and laid it on the floor next to Mama's bed. That was my home for the next four days. We we're making sure she was comfortable and in no pain.

It was Saturday and Mama had been home four days now breathing on her own. I took some personal days from work but because it's the last week of the month, I needed to go in and prepare paperwork for the next month. After being at work for two hours, my Auntie called and told me my Mama was gone. We buried her a week later.

Mom had been gone now a few months and everything seemed to be getting back to normal. I was now comfortable with where Geon and I were with our marriage. I hadn't been having any disturbing dreams and I felt like the past was finally that, the past...until one night. It's the middle of the night and as I was turning to change position in my sleep, I could feel that my pillow was soaked. Touching my hair, I realized my hair was sweating so I flipped my pillow but as I laid there it felt like I was laying on something wet. I reached down to feel the sheet that lay under me and it was soaked. I couldn't believe I sweated so much that my underwear was soaked as well.

After washing up, changing my underwear, and cleaning up my side of the bed, I laid there wondering why I was sweating so badly until I fell back to sleep. When I awoke that morning, I remembered I never followed up with my doctor. I called to make an appointment for later that day. After checking my blood levels, my doctor said my white cells has dropped more so she is scheduled me to see a specialist. I was scared and my mind is raced. I began searching the internet for answers. Waiting on the specialist was taking too long. Reading all of the many possibilities, my stress level was so high I couldn't concentrate on work or anything else. Day in and day out I found myself thinking about what could possibly be wrong with me.

I started thinking about my behavior and actions when we were separated. The fear came back. The episodes kept playing over in my head. I was afraid to fall asleep at night because that seemed to be the only time I sweat and I didn't want to wake up to wet sheets again. I went to see the Cancer and Internal Disease Specialist and I was a nervous wreck. On my way to the appointment, I was trying not to dwell on the many possibilities by listening to gospel music. I arrived and while waiting for the doctor to come in I was still singing praises all the way up until he walked in the room. Because this was my first appointment, he told me all he was going to do that today was get blood from me and run a series of test. He told me he's going to test for HIV and my head dropped. I have never been tested for this and my mind was racing again about me committing adultery and how God dealt with such sins.

Looking at me the doctor says, "You're scared."

"Yes, Sir. I am."

"You should be fine. Don't worry about it," he

said.

That's better said than done.

They drew my blood, like three tubes full and then scheduled me to return in two weeks. The car ride home was unbearable. I broke down crying, "God please forgive me for my sins. Lord, whatever it is that's wrong with me please don't let it be HIV. If not for me God but for Geon. He doesn't deserve this. I know what I did was wrong and I repent God."

The next two weeks was so stressful. Every time a commercial came on about HIV I tensed up. By the time I got to the doctor's office, I was dreading my results. I had literally slept bare naked, with no cover in order for me not to sweat.

The doctor walks in. The first thing he said is, "Well your test is negative for HIV."

I felt an enormous sigh of relief. My eyes swelled up with tears. I couldn't even hear anything else he said. I just wanted to call my husband and tell him my results. Before I left his office he said my white cells had dropped again so he wanted to do a bone marrow. Once the bone marrow was done he ruled out other possible things that could be wrong with me so he decided to just keep an eye on my cells. I had to get labs drawn every few months. My night sweats stopped and the last visit to the specialist showed that my cell count went back up. *Thank you Jesus!* The doctor explained to me that my cells just fluctuate up and down.

****

Eleven years has passed since Geon and I have been back together. Knowing that we don't have life insurance, we decided to get it. We had to take a blood test to see if we had HIV. It's been a year since I went down this path. I really didn't want to do it again but we had to be responsible and make sure our children didn't have to worry financially about us if something should happen. This made me really nervous but apparently not my husband. I wish I could be as confident as he was but I couldn't help but think about my past. It always has a way of creeping back up in my spirit.

We take all the necessary tests needed and the technician gives us a pamphlet with our own personal bar codes to check online ourselves for our results in two weeks. I stressed out for two weeks and actually decided I didn't want to know. I was going to just let the insurance company give us the news until my husband asked me about it.

"Did you check our results online?" he asked me one day.

"Nope," I said.

"What are you waiting for? Are you scared?"

I went into the computer room and logged onto the site. He came in and stood behind me, watching as I input the password and barcode for his. When I put in his email as it requested, I heard his phone notify him. He opened the email.

"This is the test you have to worry about right here," he said showing me his results. It read: *Negative.*

He had other results that probably meant he should leave those Monster Energy Drinks alone though. As I continued to put in my information, he was still standing there. When I opened my email I braced myself for the results and it read: *Negative.* Everything else they checked for was in normal range.

"How you gonna be in better health than me?" he said, giving me a kiss and leaving for work.

When he hit that door and I was alone I praised God, shouting, singing, and praying. "Thank You Jesus! Okay God. I trust You. I put this all behind me."

SEVEN

Restoration

I dwelled on my past and cried many nights while enduring child molestation, believing this was my life. Every man I would encounter I had it in my head they were looking at me wanting to have sex and I secretly looked at them as evil. When my daughter reached school age, I became more obsessed with protecting her. The fear of a man touching her consumed me. When I would drop her off at school, I'd envision a man standing in the stairwells waiting to grab her. I knew there was no one there but I was so paranoid. I wouldn't allow her to spend the night over anyone's house without me knowing who all lived in that house. She only had a select few friends that she was able to visit. I never allowed her over my father's house without me.

I did not think I would ever escape who that little girl was all those many years ago. I was someone without a voice.

I thought I had forgiven my father years ago and it wasn't until I was teaching about forgiveness in Sunday school, I realized I had not forgiven him.

My Auntie said to me one day after I shared I was going to start a molestation awareness group, "You have to forgive and you haven't."

I ignored her because in my mind I had. But while standing up there telling those folks about how important it is to forgive, God showed me not only had I not forgiven my dad but I hadn't forgiven myself. I was trying to give the people an example and the only one I could bring forth was me. I have nine sisters and brothers and out of all of us, I'm the one that doesn't visit Dad or call him. I stop by every once in a while but only for a few minutes. If it wasn't for my husband and my daughter, I would forget to call him on Father's Day or his birthday. At that moment I realized I had to acknowledge to my Auntie, "I hear you now and you were right. I haven't forgiven him."

It wasn't until God restored my own marriage that I really understood what it meant to have faith and trust in the Lord. I thought my marriage was over and I had pushed my husband away. But God kept him through it all and when the time was right. He mended what was broken. The one thing I learned from the dark path I took is that our responses determine if we win or lose. My marriage wasn't the only thing that was restored, my outlook on me being molested throughout my childhood changed.

I spent so many years distraught about my childhood and accepted that I was a victim. Now I know I am a survivor. Molestation happened to me but it is not me. The first time I realized I could help someone else was when I was in hair school and there was a young lady still in high school who also attended. One day she didn't come to school and when I asked about her, I was told she tried to commit suicide because she was being molested. I talked to this girl every day and never knew this was happening to her. I could relate to what she was going through and if I had only known, I could have shared with her that I knew how she felt. I could have helped her that day. Even though that inspired me to write and reach out, I just couldn't because I didn't want to hurt my mother by exploiting our family secrets. So I chose to put it behind me.

Within the last year I feel as though God has put it back on my heart to see this through. My mother passed away seven years ago so that couldn't be my excuse. I had to realize what happened to me was my secrets, not family secrets and they were hurting me more than helping me by holding them in. I hurt every time I hear of another child having endured molestation. Being aware there are children out there going through what I went through, and knowing that predators thrive off not being exposed because the of the victim's fears makes me angry. All too often family members don't want you telling anybody so you keep it quiet while this silent evil runs rampant through our communities at the expense of our children. I was molested for years and never felt like I could tell anyone. I felt like this was happening only to me.

I gave my life to Christ some years ago. It wasn't easy. I had to undergo a healing process from the damage of my past. A forgiving power had to take place in my spirit in order for me to even begin to heal. I'm still undergoing this process. I have to put forth continual effort to stay saved. I would be lying if I said I've got it all together. I have to fight daily through prayer and praise to overcome the demons that come against me, trying to pull me back in.

For years I've looked at my life as one not asked for but I understand now, because I found my voice, I can use it to help others find theirs. Enduring what I did doesn't just have to be a tragedy but it can also be a witness that there is life after destruction... if you want it.